For Black Men Who Need Therapy and

Never Got It By Samuel

Wright Jr.

Dedication

To my mother, Tine Wright, whose love and resilience made me who I am.
To my father, Samuel Wright Sr, whose knowledge and love guided me through life.
To Nneka, thank you for standing by my side at my lowest moments.
To my daughter, Faith. I pray my life is a betterment to yours.

"And so, lifting as we climb, onward and upward we go, struggling and striving, and hoping that the buds and blossoms of our desires will burst into glorious fruition ere long".

-Mary Church Terrell

Foreword

I was initially introduced to Samuel Wright through his journalistic work, which included a remarkable publication about Omeretta The Great. This led me to inquire about potential collaboration opportunities. It was through this exchange that I discovered we shared membership in Alpha Phi Alpha Fraternity, Incorporated, an organization that I hold in high esteem. As I got to know Samuel better, I was impressed by his intellectual prowess and extensive knowledge of global affairs and self-awareness. This book is a testament to Samuel's exceptional abilities, offering an in-depth exploration of the African diaspora. His extensive reading list, which we have discussed at length, has equipped him with the expertise necessary to author a book of this caliber. "For Black men who need therapy and never got it", this book offers a culturally relevant and timely resource. It addresses the needs of a frequently overlooked and underappreciated demographic. Samuel's writing offers invaluable insights that may prompt thousands of readers to reexamine themselves and reassess their knowledge.

Mark Sanders, Jr.,

33°, MBA CEO of

Royalty

Entertainment

President of Durr

Capital Group Best-

Selling Author

5x Award-Winning Screenwriter

2x Platinum Recording

Engineer BMI Award

Winner

Charlotte's 30 Under 30 Future Leaders

Table of Contents

Introduction

After my parents died seven months apart, I searched for answers in spiritual texts. Sometimes I feel disconnected from them, but other times, we are in sync. I learned that sharing this knowledge brought me comfort. Death provided me with the clarity and courage I needed to continue this work in the end. It gave me a new perspective on why we all need therapeutic practices to help us deal with the stresses in life.

Health experts say that healing is a journey, not a goal. None of us are completely healed. Something can still trigger us. Even specialists need support from the community.

Many of us fall into two groups: we either miss key father figures or we brace for the emptiness when they leave. On our own, we learned to *be*, mostly through trial and error. As boys, we picked up bits of traditional masculinity and cultural habits to get by from the media and society.
Without role models or traditions, the need to share knowledge with the next generation is

both important and necessary. This will help prevent them from having to unlearn toxic ways of engaging themselves and others.

How can we create something for the next generation of men? It should honor their traditions and recognize the uniqueness of their time. I want to share what helped me cope with losing my mother and then my father. My mother's spirit and creativity showed me what people can achieve. She reminded me how the mind and spirit control the body. My father's passing felt like a finality. It wasn't about his death; it marked the end of my irresponsibility too.

I could no longer count on either for advice and I realized it was my job to keep our traditions alive. I also had to step up as a role model for a new group of black men and boys, their parents, and at different points in my life, myself.

Part I

Self Awareness

Foxes, Lions, and Gorillas - A Look Into

Maneuvering Life Tools to Heal: Enneagram

Niccolo Machiavelli is one of the most controversial philosophers in the world. It might have come from your social media feed, a friend quoting the 48 Laws of Power, or a favorite movie. Even though some influencers have twisted The Prince by Machiavelli to sell love courses, it has real, practical uses. We are African American people living in a world that uses Machiavellian principles. So, we must be aware of this and adapt it to fit our needs.

Dr. Amos Wilson, a respected Black psychologist, said in his book, *The Falsification of Afrikan Consciousness*, "With an Afrikan-centered consciousness, we can take what is valuable from that tradition. We can also reject what is harmful or of little value." He highlights the importance of viewing life through an African lens. We are, whether we like it or not, descendants of African people. They used their culture to make sense of the world. No matter how much we wish to separate from this past, it still shapes our present. The past shapes our present. Machiavelli's strategies helped create the strong Western World we know today. We live in the Western World and play the same game as everyone else. But your life and actions are unique. To thrive in the game, you need to quickly understand yourself and others. Then, you can use their successful tactics.

In ancient Egypt, people looked to animals for guidance on how to live. Author Anthony Browder discusses this in his book, *Nile Valley Contributions to Civilizations*. They choose Netcher, or "Animals," for their unique qualities. Each animal represents a specific Netcher, and these traits stay the same over time. Animals like the falcon, known for clear sight, and the scarab beetle, a symbol of resurrection, were significant to the Egyptian, or Kemetian, people. They used these symbols to guide and teach others. In the Western world and Machiavelli's *The Prince* he uses a lion and a fox to show two key ideas: strength and strategy. The lion stands for strength, while the fox represents cunning. I will also include the gorilla here.

Even with its rank in the jungle, it is still a tough

opponent.

Britannica says the term "foxes" refers to more than ten species. Still, the red fox is the one we recognize best. The fox is often seen as clever and crafty. Yet, opinions on whether it symbolizes good or evil vary. Native American, Japanese, and Celtic cultures each have their own special views of the fox. Foxes are inherently good or bad, and like many aspects of life, they reflect their conditions. For you as a man, you must learn to embrace the duality within you. You're not just good or bad. Once you see how your mindset shapes your view of life, you can start to change and adapt life to meet your needs.Foxes aren't known for being dangerous hunters. They like to hunt at night, under the cover of darkness. They use different tactics, such as pouncing on their prey or playing dead before biting. This helps them secure their food. While not an outright threat, they still serve as food to someone, and as a result, hunters pursue them.

Black men start out much in the same way as a fox. You are first regarded as adorable and cuddly. Over time, you notice something. You might not feel dangerous, but others see you that way. They treat you as if you are. That awareness can twist your thoughts and make you want to lash out. But it doesn't take long to see that you're not the biggest animal in the jungle. If the hunters chose to do so, they could cut you out with little effort. You might find this scary, but you can view it through a different lens. Be yourself. Also, be adaptable in your work and home relationships. You may not be a threat to most, but the world is, and as a result, we must insulate ourselves from it. How can one maneuver through life in a way that preserves their autonomy?

Lions

Lions are known as the kings of the jungle. They are strong and fierce animals. Compared to the wider world, these mammals seem to have it all. Even so, the toughest lions depend on their shells to protect them from predators. Compared to other hunters, they usually have a much lower kill rate. Lions usually depend on packs to eat.
Alone, they don't have the speed or flexibility to be dominant.

Many of us brothers show dominant traits but few of us have the legal support and networks to protect ourselves from life's threats. Ask the strongest black men you know if they often feel powerful. They often work in silos and miss out on success. They struggle to connect with other black men. Plus, they also find it tough to know when to disguise themselves for safety. For some of us, we could use more courage, and for others of us, we could use more caution. Lions often think and act based on the Enneagram. It's helpful to recognize that feeling inadequate sometimes is okay. Accept that you can't change the limits tied to race and gender.

Gorillas

Very rarely do people sit and think about the characteristics of a gorilla. Gorillas are the largest primates in the animal kingdom. Unlike lions and foxes, they do not dominate or hide from their prey. Often seen as peaceful, they act only when their family or territory is in danger. This behavior supports their calm reputation. They are usually peaceful, but they are also among the strongest animals on Earth. Their arms and upper bodies can be quite intimidating.

You can see strength on the outside, but inner strength is what holds your life together. As you grow, you will see that you can be strong and attract attention without being aggressive or bossy.

Enneagram

The Enneagram, created by Oscar Ichazo, has 144 statements. These statements help you become more self- aware. The nine personality types and their wings shape our behavior. They split the traits into three groups: action, thinking, and feeling. They also reveal how we react under stress or when we grow.

Know yourself before trying to disguise who you are in front of others. Self-help and therapy talks often encourage us to feel our emotions and learn why that is the case. This is especially helpful for you, a Black man who may need therapy but hasn't sought it yet. Skip the lengthy talks and common personality tests. Take a moment to Google the Enneagram test.

For you, black man, I would take 40 minutes of my time and take this test. I would answer with complete sincerity, as though my life depended on it. Then, I'd take a moment to think about what it shows me about myself. I remind myself that only I can define who I am. My traits are neither good nor bad; they are strengths and things I can improve. First, I give myself grace; then I sit with the feeling. Take a moment to recognize your defense mechanism against change. Let it simmer in your thoughts before you try to turn off that mental chatter.

Take a moment if you're still trying to process all this. It's tough to hear that no matter your good deeds, you may have harmed others without knowing. Doesn't feel too hot, I know, but like we said, you aren't threatening by nature any more than you are evil by nature. That doesn't change how you are, nor does it change the effect it has on your existence in this very real material world. Now that you see your flaws, you can start thinking about how to show yourself better. You can also find ways to hide those traits to get by.

Some people say it's all about being true to yourself, even when facing opposition. But, as we mentioned earlier, a quick look around might show that you may not be strong enough mentally to do that. You might belong to one or more of these groups: looking for financial stability, seeking mental or physical stability, or both. This means you may not have the right mix to weather life's storms. If this sounds like you, then learn to hide your weaknesses. Focus on showing your strengths. This way, you can gain advantages in many areas. If you understand finance and feel stable, you're ready for the Lion segment. Unlike school, you can scroll ahead. Everyone else, sit tight and roll with me a little longer.

Find out your personality type. Identify the addictions that go with them. Be mindful of the actions you take. Before moving on to other black men, you must first remember that no matter where you are, who you are, as Jay said. Too many of us wear the mask without remembering what we put it on for and who we are underneath it. Your goal isn't to be a method actor like some rappers, athletes, or fathers. Instead, focus on knowing your faults. Get into character when it's needed. Just like many actors or artists use physical cues or sounds to inspire action, you should do the same. Think of work, social gatherings, and events as nighttime. You are the fox, looking to corner your meal. Sometimes, you may need to play dead to survive and fight another day. But remember, the goal is peace of mind. We don't have to keep warring like our fathers, uncles, and brothers did. They were lions, but we can choose a different path.

Know Thyself

Many associate the saying "know yourself" with Greek philosophy or the Bible. But if you're a Black man, think of its Kemetic or Egyptian roots. This saying connects to your freedom. Understanding yourself goes beyond knowing your triggers and how to handle them. It explores how memory shapes our identities. It also shows how these memories influence our purpose in life.

Dr. Wade Nobles is a Black psychologist and educator. He has shaped black education for over forty years. In his article, "Extended Self: Rethinking the So-Called Negro Self Concept," he examines our origins as Americanized Africans. He highlights our communal tradition, which values teamwork and collaboration. Nobles references African philosopher John Mbiti, stating, "The key to understanding the traditional African view of self is the belief that I am because we are, and because we are, I am (cf: Mbiti, 1970)." The concept of Ubuntu means "I am because we are." It highlights our strong belief in community. We carry the memory of those who are no longer with us in everything we do.

Nobles also embrace Mbiti's view of time. He sees it as a two-dimensional lane. For these people, they must experience time to make it real." Kalumba states in "A New Analysis of Mbiti's 'The Concept of Time'" that we have only experienced the past and present. 1, March 2005: 11-20). Time is continuous. Events from the past shape our present. This is different from the linear view common in the Western world. Accepting this gives us many things to consider for our self-governance.

We carry the DNA of those who came before us. Their spiritual and emotional marks influence much of what we do. If you doubt this idea, look into research on how epigenetics and trauma affect our DNA and change us.

Research in the article "Transgenerational transmission of environmental information in C Elegans" shows that trauma can change the worms' DNA for up to fourteen generations.

The past shapes our present and will impact our children's future, whether we like it or not, even if we don't have kids. We need to adopt a community-based mindset. This means we support each other. We also focus on raising strong children for the future.

Be Yourself

"Let us do our duty to ourselves, and redeem our name among men, and thus establish a position, based upon our own exertions, which shall be an inheritance to our children." - *Martin Delany (The Condition, Elevation, Emigration, and Destiny of the Colored People of the United States, 1852)*

When the term Pan-Africanism comes up, most people think of Marcus Garvey, which is fitting. He is often seen as the father of Pan-Africanism. He believed Black people should embrace their African roots. Some see his call to return to Africa as outdated. Last year, I started reading about Martin R. Delany. He plays a major role as a Black leader, and people see him as a key figure in Nationalism and Pan-Africanism. Delany believed that the success of Black people worldwide was linked together. He felt that no matter where we were on Earth, we belonged to our nation.

That belief over time would grow into what professor Maggie Morehouse calls, "The

African Diaspora Theory". In her article, "African Diaspora Theory: Here, There, and Everywhere," she says that diaspora means a community formed by people who move." Dr. Joseph Harris was among the first scholars to write about the African

Diaspora. He shared his thoughts on the topic with readers:

The African Diaspora isn't one event. It's a continuous journey with many migrations to various parts of the world.

The culture of Black people is similar around the world, but each region has its own special traits.

The connection to Africa remains evident in our spiritual, musical, and cultural actions.

As black men, we need to see each other as part of a shared story. We shouldn't view ourselves as having skin color in common. America is our home,, and it has been good to us in a lot of ways. Even though it's familiar, it remains a tough place for us. If we don't show compassion, we start to see each other negatively. We must recognize our shared struggles. This can lead to worse feelings toward other Black people too. We are part of a global family of black people. This includes those in North America, South America, Africa, and beyond. If you're Black American,

Caribbean American, or African American, you are part of the diaspora. This means you share in both the benefits and challenges of being part of that group. If you are from Africa, there is a beauty in being able to go directly back home to your village and touch the soil. Last year in Africa, I fell for the dream of a mythical land of milk and honey with great enthusiasm.

But soon, I realized it wasn't real. I learned that each African country felt the effects of colonialism. What matters more is the mindset and ideals of the people who live there.

As Black Americans, we may forget the struggles and beauty of our African brothers. We also ignore the flaws in our own country. Just because we managed to avoid being on the opposite side of the power struggle doesn't mean we are any better off. Until we can look at each other's situations as our own, we won't win. We know how important it is for us to understand who we are, but now it is time for us to be who we are: Americanized Africans. We must walk in truth. This made me think of what Martin Delaney said: "We are a nation within a nation. We are American citizens by birth, not by adoption. This is our native land: we know no other."

We are survivors of one of the world's greatest disasters, called the Maafa. Our genius and beauty survived enslavement, separation, and destruction. You can find physical monuments of this all around us. We are the only ones who can change our conditions. This affects everyone, no matter how you view yourself. We are responsible for the future of our people, and if we can make it happen in America, we can do it anywhere.

Black Doug Funny: A Case Study

Perspectives: Integral Theory by

Ken Wilbur

I grew up in the 90s, watching Nickelodeon.
Shows like "Hey Arnold" and "Clarissa Explains
it All" shaped our views. They showed both
good and bad themes. One of my favorites was
always Doug. He was a dreamer who loved
writing, art, and music. He kept a journal to
share his dreams and life. He hoped for a future
where others would see his talent and romantic
wishes. Doug yearned for Patti. We couldn't say
exactly why, but we knew his pursuit lacked
inspiration.

Many of us felt that someone had wronged
Doug. We wanted to avoid his fate. But, without
his skills and street smarts, we became mini
Doug Funnies in our communities. You may be
too cool to say it now, but if we dug through
many of your pictures, we'd see a much milder,
nicer version of you there. We'd see a smile
devoid of cynicism and filled with hope. After
years of seeking love, many turned to the red
pill cult. Some joined willingly, but others felt

pressured. In college, I noticed something strange. Brothers who liked crime gained great respect.

Meanwhile, gentle men were often the butt of jokes for everyone. Caught between rebellion and fear, I turned to Tomollo Rasi's key book, The Rational Male, for guidance. Smart and insightful, I connected with its ideas and felt enlightened. Yet, I worried that fully embracing them might betray my inner voice. Still, it offered a cure for my rising cynicism.

Many of you may relate to this. You might have found comfort in red pill ideas like Plate Theory or Sexual Marketplace Value. These ideas may seem calming, but they only hide a bigger issue: a raging fire. Cynicism makes us think that being right matters more than working together. That's the real danger. It's ok to live in a world of realities, but never forget that you shape your reality with the lens you look through. Embracing these concepts is akin to avoiding the plank in your eye for the speck in your sister's. In short, my brother, it's cool to understand hypergamy and the reality that people are selfish. Living in constant pessimism about women isn't helpful. We often rely on generalizations instead. It's good to support black brothers in bettering themselves. They should focus on both their physical and mental health. It is not ok to tell them that it is ok to not marry women and play the game forever. It's even crazier for my brother to say that young men find relationships with women too hard. In a world where all relationships are stressful, that seems off.

Ask anyone if it's tougher to deal with parents and relatives than with a coworker or spouse. You'll find it's more about perspective than you might think. But what's happened is we allowed the cynicism and comedy we used for relief to become our permanent canvas and now we have a generation of men who hate women but love having sex with them. In fear of being like Doug Funnie, many of us turn into Roger Klotz. We fumble our relationships and end up alone.

This chapter may turn some off, but it's the real. A therapist could cost you hundreds just to tell you that you're holding on to a story that no longer serves you. I can help you with this for a much lower fee. Whoever you were, or rather, whoever people thought you were, is not as important as who you choose to be from now on. A star knows he's a star before anyone else does, and they don't need the sun/son to confirm it.

Take comfort, black man. Those who judged you the most were often in pain themselves. They put their insecurities and unfair judgments on you. They acted like it was their right. You might have felt that way. You were always superior, like a child trying to win over a parent at bedtime. The parent knows inside that beneath all their crying, they know the truth. You knew it as well, and you know it now. We need each other to survive in this world. The best way to make a difference is by working together. Posting endless memes that justify abuse against women won't help. So for you,, my guy, the only exercise I ask of you involves you journaling your feelings. For those averse to writing, you can record yourself. In any case, speak to yourself about the painful interactions you had with the women in your life.

Integral Theory, created by philosopher Ken Wilbur, is a valuable framework to explore. In "Introduction to Integral Theory and Practice," Ken Wilbur talks about how the world sees men and women. He uses a four-quadrant model to explain this connection. The model groups knowledge into four types: subjective, objective, intersubjective, and interobjective. The framework then dives into stages of moral development. In this framework, two main ideas stand out. These are agency and communion, often applied to both men and women.

In *In A Different Voice, Carol Gilligan explains that "male logic" focuses on autonomy, justice, and rights. So, "female logic" emphasizes relationships, care, and responsibility. Men tend toward agency; women tend toward communion." Gilligan introduces four stages of moral development. Both men and women can reach the highest level. This level includes four stages: preconventional, conventional, postconventional, and integrated. As a man, aim to understand your connections with women. We may hear different voices, but our goal is the same.

To unpack your ideas and feelings, start by connecting with yourself. Then, reach out to others. Shift away from anger and judgment, and move toward acceptance and empathy. You don't have to agree with how others live or think. Accepting different views can make you more influential in the end. Also, focus on letting go of others' opinions and valuing your own. We often listen to podcast hosts who tap into our trauma. They share generalizations that we accept as truth, even if we don't realize it. Value your viewpoint, but know that others may critique it. You need to confront your thoughts head-on. If they aren't useful anymore, let them go.

LGBTQ+IA Brothers

Your pain is as real as the catalyst for the pain experienced by most of our women. Men, feeling insecure, tried to control masculinity. They wanted you to feel inferior for being yourself. You felt hurt, angered, and betrayed by those you trusted. Like the red pill brothers, you let that pain shape your views. You hid your anger behind clever theories and ideologies. You focus on all black men, not specific ones. Like our sisters, you sometimes turn to cynicism and anger for comfort. Seek healthy relationships with healed men. They can offer true friendship. I understand your point. I can't tell you what to do since your struggle is unique. But know this: some men see your humanity. They view it as vital to our freedom. I ask that you remain open to it and believe in its possibility. To give more insight on this, I'd like to explain the concept of Social Dominance Theory.

Jim Sidanius and Felicia Protto developed Social Dominance Theory. It explains why some individuals hold more privilege and power than others. Social Dominance Theory (SDT) explains how societies create group-based hierarchies. It states that dominant groups receive more benefits, like good jobs and health care. Meanwhile, subordinate groups face more hardships, such as poor housing and health.

This shows that even within groups, there are in-groups and out-groups. These groups can discriminate against each other. This makes some feel less than if they don't follow certain ideas and beliefs. Heterosexual black men can face discrimination, violence, and exclusion. This often comes from other black men who support hyper masculine ideals. You might find this surprising. It might look like we're part of the problem because we are straight black men. But our struggle goes deeper than that. We both agree the issue isn't our sexual orientation. It's the belief that all black men should think and act alike. We fight for all individuals to respect and value each other's differences. Knowing why some black men want to dominate others can help us change this trend. This awareness helps us find words like privilege hoarding and heteronormativity. It also guides us in teaching the next generation of black boys how to be real revolutionaries.

One tool for this is the Social Dominance Scale. Sidanius and Pratto created it. For the sake of convenience, I am attaching an example of one adapted for your personal use. Higher SDO scores mean a greater desire to control others. Lower scores show a preference for equality. Take the assessment yourself and then have your male friends do the same. Use the data as a talking point for follow-up conversations.

Father Time Mother Nature

"Someone once said that every man is trying to live up to his father's expectations or make up for his mistakes." - Barack Obama (The Audacity of Hope)

Society's demands feel like a constant struggle, pushing Black Men throughout life. For those of us with fathers, we had a man at home. He may or may not have value emotions. Instead, he focused on providing for us. This made submission and obedience feel like a military routine. Those without a father often learned to live without him.

They might resent him or eventually find forgiveness.

There are two dominant thoughts on why this is so. One leans more towards nature while the other leans towards nurture. Many statistics show that what we see and hear influences us. We didn't need anyone to explain that herd mentality made us rush to the streets, sports, or try to fit in with our peers. We knew that the environment that raised us, or rather failed to do so, is why so many of us know better but choose worse.

Often, our greatness and maturity go unrecognized. Our mistakes loom larger while our areas of growth and strength are often forgotten by even our closest of friends. Take for instance the black father conversation. According to a 2013 article from the CDC, *Father's Involvement With*

Their Children United States, 2006-2010, black fathers are the most active fathers out of all the groups surveyed, eating with their children at higher rates than most while also having the highest rates of parental help for their children whether we live together or not. (Jones & Mosher, 2013).

Despite how hard black men have been working to change the narrative, society seems to only show our flaws.
However in order for us to move forward, we need to understand the trauma we've inherited. We must also recognize the signs. That temper didn't come from nowhere. That timidity didn't arise overnight, and that desire to conquer every woman you see isn't an anomaly. While many solid examples exist, a significant number of us fail to honor families and women.

Psychologist James Hillman wrote *The Soul Code* in 1996. It's based on Plato's myth of Er. This myth says we have a guiding spirit before birth. This spirit calls us to fulfill our life's mission. The acorn theory says we all have hidden potential inside us. This potential waits to grow, but it often stays unseen, even by us. No matter what society says, we all have an inner voice guiding us toward success. Various religions call it a different thing, but whether you believe it or not is not the point. All of us have a voice that only we can hear inside of us, and when we are honest with ourselves, we know what to do. We don't know how it will turn out, and that is where life's distractions and excuses come in. You, my brother, might still be dealing with anger toward one or both parents. Acknowledging this soon will help you feel freer. Instead of blaming others for their mistakes, try to forgive them for their ignorance. Focus on how you can become the person you want to be.

Some of you might say your parents aren't the source of your pain. But I challenge you to think about it. Our need for others often comes from how we were raised. As children, we looked to our parents for love, acceptance, and safety. Humans want acceptance, connection, and safety. Many of our vices come from wanting to fulfill our needs. This includes gluttony, gambling, drugs, and lust. Psychology has interesting terms for these theories. But we must address the real wounds of mother and father. At some point, you have to make peace with the fact that this person you call a parent is a person. Their desires pushed them, and their vices troubled them, like yours do. If they hadn't worked on their flaws like you do, it likely took them longer to see how their actions affected them.

To avoid that being your fate, sit with the following truths:

No one, including your mate, can meet all your needs, nor should they. They can only add to the feelings you already have. If you can't manage your feelings, they can't correct them any more than you can. You are the captain of your fate and master of your soul.

Uncontrolled desire, whether it's for money, sex, or attention,, will bring about your demise. Nothing—no sex, fame, or wealth—will make you feel complete. Only knowing you are valued, loved, and special can bring true fulfillment. That, my boy, first starts with you and then is reflected in the people around you.

You are more like your parents than you will ever know. We copy the actions of those we hang out with. If you don't notice this, you risk repeating their behavior. The acorn theory claims genetics has limits. It also considers mirror neurons and traits passed through DNA. Know yourself and one aspect of that comes from knowing where you came from.

Epigenetic research shows that trauma can be passed down through generations. This means we may inherit some vices from our parents. I realized that his strong need for validation from peers was also in me. It wasn't just a coincidence. I also had to accept that I was not my father, and that my lived experiences were not his and so I had a choice. My father grew up in the projects of Atlanta. He was a genius. He had the skills to connect with other students. I had to work hard to develop that ability myself. I had to realize that it wasn't my job to replicate my father's circumstances, but rather decide to be my own voice. That awakening was freeing, but I won't act as if it came instantly. It took me years to make peace with this fact and even longer to simply accept what I knew to be true all along.

Losing my mother and reflecting on times I felt neglected has taught me more than I thought it would. Many of us may not realize it, but our unmet needs often come from childhood. So, while I won't say we all have a father or mother wound, these early issues can shape our desires. If you had a father who was present but not really there, you likely missed important lessons. This is similar for those without a father. Your relationship may affect your desire to learn these lessons on your own. This is your reminder: it's never too late to take charge and learn the skills you need to thrive. For those who learn best from video, YouTube University is for you.

If you need hands-on help, check for local meetups. You can also ask people in your network. There might be men and women who know how to do specific tasks. In your small or larger network, there's likely someone right in front of you who can help.

If you have a mother wound, you'll need a gentle approach based on your situation. Communion principles help you understand your feelings. First, look at the primary and secondary emotions involved. Then, ask yourself why you feel that way. This approach can help you spot and recognize your patterns. Anger is often seen as a primary response because it hits us fast. But beneath that outburst, many emotions await exploration. It's important for you, as a Black man, to express your pain and childhood feelings. Doing so will help you move on. You are angry because your feelings were hurt and you couldn't change it. You are angry because you were neglected and that made you seek revenge. No matter if your childhood was good or bad, we all carry some pain that shapes us. The more we know about it, the better we can prevent it from harming our current and future relationships.

No, Don't Let That Hurt Go King: How to Channel Pain Tools : Socratic Questions for Cognitive Restructuring

Sometimes, the best thing you can do is remember the experiences that made you the angriest. I am by no means telling you that holding on to resentment is healthy. A better view of the situation, along with a focused action to achieve it, can help.

Cognitive Restructuring

Yes, this idea appears in many therapy fields. But you can grasp it without seeing a therapist. People who hurt you, like that employer or the guy who disrespected you, help you grow. But remember, the events matter less than the story you tell yourself about them. Events do happen, but how we see them affects how we feel and in turn how we act. We often blame others for our pain. Their actions might hurt us, but we can create a whole story around it that stops us from healing.

Yes, ole girl broke up with you, but she doesn't have the power to hurt you. In fact, your ego is more hurt than you are when you really get to the heart of it. More than likely, things weren't productive and that end helped you both. But if the story you told yourself was one filled with hurt and then anger, that anger's potency is slightly tamer. At first, anger feels justified. The results we achieve can make us think it is. But later, that emptiness shows us another truth. But that's for a later time. One step at a time. In short, change the lens you are using towards the situation from one of a victim to one of a hero. You are on a solo mission to prove to yourself that nothing can break you. The fire inside you is your only proof of who you truly are.

The Batman Effect

Rachel E. White and Stephanie Carlson (2016) popularized the idea in their article, "The Batman Effect: Improving Perseverance in Young Children." Their research focused on how children completed a repetitive task. They found that kids who imagined themselves as Batman were better at persevering. The goal is to learn how to reshape your thoughts and feelings about unfair situations. To be your hero, embrace your role like a method actor. This means tapping into what psychologists call the Batman Effect. Like Kobe Bryant became Mamba, Beyonce became Sasha Fierce, and David Goggins found Goggins, you need to stand out too. Use the right thoughts to guide your journey to save yourself. Shifting your focus from saving others helps you realize something important. It was never really about proving yourself to them. It was about confirming who you are when you're alone.

To get into character, you need regular practice. You should have a cue that triggers your character when you hear or see it. For some, visualizing the event is a strong cue. Later, it becomes an anchor to remind them they are in character. You can picture the event in your mind. Then, for deeper character building, try imagining it while looking in the mirror.

Seeing your mind change your face and body shows the power of visualization. Some people need a physical cue or item to represent their attitude. This could be something small, like a photo or a totem. Kobe Bryant once talked about his "kill list" from high school. Michael Jordan also shared how negative press pushed him to prove his critics wrong. Clothing can also serve as a cue. Batman, Superman, and most heroes wear costumes and symbols we recognize.

In these cases, view the above suggestions as flexible options. They can help spark that engine inside you. When it is time to get into character, focus on the item and visualize the outcome you want.

Next, add the accelerant. For me, music in particular, music from artists like 2Pac and Kanye West provides that emotion I need. For you, affirmations may help and provide that information. Talk to yourself positively, like you would answer an interviewer's question. I enjoy talking to myself like I'm in an interview. It gives me motivation and hope to succeed. Mix that vision with the right words. You'll get the energy and emotion needed to face big challenges.

Black Bayle (The Bayle Enigma)

During the pandemic, I finally became an adjunct professor at my alma mater. I taught World History. One of my favorite subjects to teach was the Enlightenment Era.

Among all the thinkers, Pierre Bayle stood out to me. He was a French writer and thinker. He is best known for his unique outlook on life. He often presents arguments from both sides equally. This can make it hard for readers to know his true opinion.

For black people, especially black Americans, the idea of double consciousness is real. We often navigate this tricky balance. In corporate settings, we code-switch. We prioritize our families and friends over our fears and emotions. Sometimes, we feel like imposters. But for many of us, we struggle with a framework for the feelings and more so struggle with what to do with it. Black man, let me be real: You show the different views Bayle mentioned— those of a lawyer and a reporter.

As a lawyer, your role is to share the facts and make your case. This means being honest with yourself, family, friends, and colleagues about the world. You might be among the few who can do this. A modern term that fits this idea is "intellectual sparring partner," which comes from Sahil Bloom. In your group, your role is to present clear cases based on logic and facts. This helps others reach their full potential. You should know that a lawyer's job is to share information with a goal. Sometimes, showing facts as we see them helps achieve that goal.

This way of thinking has limits. Sometimes, the truth we tell ourselves isn't what we really need. Many men today seem cynical about the world. They act like these problems are new, but they've been around forever. Money is always necessary. Women can be challenging. The world is often dangerous. But, this truth might not apply to everyone.

That is when we need the reporter lens.

As a reporter, your job is to tell things as they are, removing your personal bias as much as possible. Writing about your feelings shows that mindset. It also means being open with the people around you. Share what you see and hear from them. As a lawyer, your goal was to share the facts in a way that keeps the relationship strong. However, sometimes you must also embrace the truth, even if it's uncomfortable. This honesty helps everyone grow. As a black man, your role is to navigate contradictions. You can bring both relief and grief as needed. Remember, your true intentions may often be misunderstood.

This mindset is essential for your personal and collective development. We live in a world filled with people who have different beliefs and opinions. Some of these may not make sense to us. Your awareness level affects how you relate to the struggles of those around you. You might quietly sense the pain they face at work and home. Society often takes from them every day. If you don't know, hearing their abuse and exploitation stories can be overwhelming.

The Enlightenment era is interesting. We credit men for recognizing that people deserve equal treatment. For women, who often faced unfairness, it was clear that everyone should be free to be themselves. In my personal life, I meet brothers from many backgrounds. They have different views on society and faith, but I enjoy learning from them. I also fight for their right to share their ideas. If you believe the black man is god, I respect it. If you don't believe there is a god, I understand how you could feel that way.

Most of all, I champion your right to feel that way and share it with whoever you choose. I can also question those ideas with love. I balance criticism with curiosity. Later, we will explore why changing your friend circles is key for balance in life. The main point is that your goal should be to grow until your old beliefs feel unfamiliar. We often pride ourselves on staying the same. But as we grow and learn, our views should change. As we change directions, our understanding should shift as well.

Windows Of The World Tools: Johari Window Model

My dad was an intellectual, just like me. His training combined both school and self-study. His outside reading built on his foundation. It helped him apply these theories and concepts to himself and others like him. During one chat, he talked about the Johari Window Model. This model divides human understanding and self-awareness into four categories. The two main areas are what we know about ourselves and what we don't. They also include what we see and what is hidden from us and others. Most of us have traits that we recognize in ourselves. Others see these traits too. We often call these traits our personality. It is the part of us we openly see and know. But the true power comes from that side of ourselves that we don't know exists.

Referred to by some as the shadow side, it is here where we must do our most work. You have traits you know about but often hide. Sometimes, you even hide them from yourself. You fear these traits could make you irredeemable. You can be forgiven for anything. Just understand what forgiveness really means. The hard truth is that to know yourself and make amends, you must face your true duality. You are not as good as you think you are and not as bad as you or others may think either. Your negative traits are part of you. Accept them. When you try to hide them, they stand out more. The brighter you try to cover them, the more others will notice. Your shadow and your blind side are two sides of the same coin. They show the need for both outside and inside work.

As an educator for life, I often reflect on my past with students. I think about how I viewed their behaviors. As a man, I've faced similar challenges. I've realized we often swing to extremes. We either praise ourselves too much for what we should do or harshly judge ourselves for small mistakes. The other side of that is not being able to celebrate your wins and overlooking your flaws as well. To truly integrate and connect with yourself, you must see clearly. Your actions show who you are more than anything else. If you think you're a "good guy," but your actions are manipulative, something is off. If you see yourself as a man's man but find it hard to open up and get support, something isn't right. We have to be able to see ourselves as who we really are.

Caveat: We are what we do, but only we can know the part of self that remains hidden from all. We are so complex that we shouldn't get caught up in the idea of self. Our idea of self may not be seen often, but it's important. Keep it close during tough times. Your core view of self will guide you.

Your blind spots can be unconscious. They include things you say or do that affect how others feel about you.
Understanding these is important for your healing journey. If you don't want to join a group, try the Harvard Implicit

Bias Test. It can help you see your hidden biases. This way, you'll be more informed and aware of the world. Elements of our biases are grounded in the realities we accept, but that doesn't make you bad as much as uninformed.

If you were paying attention earlier, you know that tests like the Enneagram help us discover our shadows. I suggest using tests like the Clifton Strengths Assessment and the Gallup Test. Use the test information to highlight strengths. View areas for growth as opportunities, not weaknesses.

The Memory Mandate

Called an accomplishment journal or brag book, it's one of my favorite tools. In a world that often makes us feel inadequate without our highlight reel, it helps me shine. In my case, I didn't start to do a brag book. During the pandemic, I felt like I was changing my life. Those moments really needed attention. I decided to clip images and upload proof of my achievements. I put them in a document called **Personal Motivation**. This helps me during days when I doubt myself.

Gratitude is a trait many people find hard to practice. There are several reasons it often gets ignored. For much of my life, I had trouble tracking my achievements. It felt like I was running on a treadmill, always climbing but never reaching a finish line. I constantly felt inadequate. I compared myself to others who seemed happy. They received the praise I wanted so much. Once I started looking for small wins, they felt bigger. I published articles that got steady views and comments. I also watched my SEO rank climb. I needed to keep track of them and reflect on them frequently.

Earlier, we talked about how you can reshape your self- thoughts to grow. This idea also fits with this exercise.

Each time you achieve a goal, you strengthen how you see yourself. You also surprise others with this new image.

Your mask is on to the world and so you need to document it to stay in character. We often focus on memories close to home. In this busy world, we forget our biggest moments. We also dwell on our lowest points, which keeps us stuck in a loop.

I typically don't promote specific ideas. But I want you to reflect on your life. It's better to be a bit arrogant than to feel small while pretending to be humble. Everyone around you may remind you of your average status. But instead, focus on your inner greatness. Reflect on your wins and embrace who you are. The quickest way to lose enthusiasm is to hope others feel it. People often don't have the background to appreciate a win. Even clear victories can spark insecurities before bringing joy.

Knowing that, you should know who you are and relish that fact in your lowest moments. Talking about our wins can boost our emotional security. But it can also invite envy and jealousy. This makes us targets for negative feelings. Social media is a great way to promote our businesses and share our progress. But if we misuse it, we might attract those looking to take advantage of us. Write down your wins. Reflect on them and celebrate with friends and family. Remember, the results will come, whether you want them to or not.

The

Warrior

World

Perspectiv

es:

Bushido

Bushido, as Tim Clark explains in his article "Samurai and the Bushido Code," is a code of conduct. Ancient samurai, Japan's warriors, followed it during times of war and peace.

The code has eight character traits:

- Rectitude
- Courage
- Mercy
- Politeness
- Honesty or sincerity
- Honor
- Loyalty
- Self-control

An unwritten code for warriors, it is now a

leading school of thought. It influences many areas of life, from the boardroom to the dojo. If you've come this far in life, you likely adopted these principles. You might have found structure at home, in the military, or in a fraternity. No matter where you learned them, these principles are essential in life.

In 2022, I started practicing a mixed martial art called 52 Blocks in Atlanta. It helped me understand myself better as an adult. As a kid, I practiced Tae Kwon Do. This Korean martial art emphasized kicks, with some punching variations. I spent more than ten years in classes at the Atlanta Tae Kwon Do Academy. I learned the 5 commandments and built my skills. But only in the last two years did I see the purpose of my training. That's when I started to enjoy its benefits.

52 Blocks added boxing to my skills. It changed how I think about fighting and put me back in the learning zone. More than anything though, it made me aware of my inner warrior inside. As men, strong or weak, we all have it inside of us, and it is a matter of life and death for us to find him and tame him. One of my favorite comparisons is between two types of warriors: a soldier and a thug. A soldier, no matter how we feel about him, often aims to help others. In contrast, a thug focuses only on his own desires. Choosing a moral compass over a spiritual one is crucial. It helps you become a man of service in a world where many seek service but shy away from commitment.To help my guy heal, start training. Focus on building mental, physical, and especially spiritual discipline. This will prepare you for anything life

throws your way.

Though I led with mental, your spiritual mindset (not religious) is the start. When I chose to take on 52, I realized I needed to be a student again. I knew I had to improve myself for my own sake first, then for others. Your spirit can not be weak in a world that seeks to subject you to unspeakable cruelty. Your spirit also cannot be dark in a world of unfathomable kindness and innocence. Your spirit should be grounded in principles but flexible in how you apply them. This means loving others, but sometimes you must love yourself more. To become that person, read books that build a warrior mindset. Watch motivational videos that inspire you to reach for the stars. Also, look at history for men and women who stood strong in tough times. Once you know what you want to see, you can start training your mind and body the right way.

To sync your mind and body, you need regular physical training. For me, that means combat. I respect the skills non-combat sports offer. But I also encourage everyone to try combat sports, both youth and adults. Nothing trains your mind and body like learning to punch, wrestle, and kick. Nothing boosts your confidence like knowing you can stand up to stronger fighters. Fighting less-skilled opponents helps us train and support others. In contrast, facing better fighters boosts our fighting spirit. This obsession drives us to become stronger protectors.

Projection Hub (Social Media)

Perspective: Cultural Cognition

Theory

Many thinkers believe we shouldn't take in so
many thoughts, opinions, and views all at once.
The endless stream of information, lies, and
temptations brings us to the brink of a major
mental health crisis. As black men, we often
defend our long use of this tool. We say it gives
us information, motivation, and promotion. But
we overlook how it makes us desire things we
shouldn't and value what isn't real. It mostly
ignores how it replaces our true thoughts. It
swaps healthy ideas for false ones and
projections. Reading and staying active are
important to me, but they can't replace my
biggest vice. What's more dangerous is not just
how much we rely on it for marketing and
entertainment. It's also how smoothly it
suggests ideas and concepts to us.

Echo chambers refer to social situations where
people intentionally align themselves with
people who feel the same, willfully ignoring the
thoughts of those who don't and excluding them

from their group. Epistemic bubbles on the other hand refer to social situations where people aren't exposed to outside ideas unintentionally. It's important for us to explore ideas that don't always match our friends' views, both online and in real life. Your friend group might be full of brothers from the trenches. They may believe that men should embrace their aggressive side, and that idea has its place. Try to learn from both men and women who seek diplomatic ways to handle conflict. It can also help to befriend those who share the same values.

Your timeline likely has many familiar characters. If you identify with a political or religious label, you might feel your way of life is the best. This is due to the constant flow of information. Start changing the algorithm's energy by looking for views that differ from yours. If you enjoy content from Andrew Tate and David Goggins, try exploring other creators. Check out Jason Wilson, Dewayne Noel, F.D. Signifier, Marc Lamont Hill, and Olayemi Olurin. They discuss topics you might not usually consider. If you enjoy content like this, check out channels like Prager U. You should also read writers such as Adolph L. Reed and Thomas Chatteron Williams. They all share a common goal: an America and a world where we can express our ideas respectfully. They also work to find common ground on issues that benefit everyone.

I have friends with different religious and political beliefs. I try to support them. Friendship means sharing ideas, even if we don't agree. We need to be open to different perspectives. Most importantly, we must avoid cognitive dissonance just because we love our views. We also need to notice when our thoughts aren't truly ours. Sometimes, we become victims, absorbing content that excuses our failures. A great way to do this is to take the Cultural Cognition Quiz by David Ropeik, a well-known professor and author. After you know your cultural outlook, you can improve how you connect with others. It shows you which online communities to follow. This can help broaden your perspective.

Spiritual Thoughts Pt 1

At some point, something hurtful happened to you. A loved one said, "Things happen for a reason, don't question God." They didn't mean any harm, but you likely felt dismissed. You may have thought the person was being thoughtless. I get it. They meant to say don't let this pain make you forget God is here. It's not our job to understand the why or how. Instead, we should grow from it.

In our community, we often face life's pain. Some turn to drugs or other vices to cope. Others may lean too much into religious zealotry to hide their feelings. Both ideas are clear when we consider the pain we experience or see each day. It's a natural way to cope. As men, we must face reality. We shouldn't let nihilism take hold. Also, we need to release our logical side. This way, cynicism won't control us. Our brains are powerful tools. They help us see that 1+1 equals 2. We often forget that information only makes sense when we observe it through our senses. Death and pain are feelings that go beyond our usual understanding. Trying to make sense of them can lead to narrow judgments that lack context. In other words my guy, there is some information you simply won't know, can't comprehend, and don't need to know. Let go of that need to know and explain everything. If scientists can't explain everything, why should we feel the need to? After all, even the smartest minds have been puzzled by some things.

On the other hand, we should always embrace science, logic, and practicality. We must avoid religious extremism. How can you know that is God's will? Even more, hasn't he given us dominion over the Earth, giving us the powers to govern the day to day events in our life? If so, our failures are indicative of our failure to follow God's orders and even more our tyranny. That mindset leads us into darkness. It takes away our control over our lives. We also bypass our spiritual responsibility here on Earth. Spirituality and religion can offer comfort and support growth, especially for Black men. However, they should never excuse a lack of effort. Some events on Earth and in space remain a mystery. This is true for everyone, regardless of their beliefs in spirituality or religion. This holds true even with our current models, called the Newtonian Paradigm.

Spiritual

Thoughts Pt

2

Many of us find it hard to accept religious ideas.
We often question tough issues and may reject
the need for faith in mystical beliefs. You might
think we are gods and that a Creator doesn't
exist. You may point to many problems in the
world that seem ignored. You use these issues
as proof that nothing is there to stop the
wrongs. You might be someone who believes,
sometimes too much, that everything is part of
God's plan. You may feel powerless to change
anything.

These schools of thought have existed for years.
They fall under two categories: transcendence and
immanence.
Transcendents think the creator is above all
creation. They see the creator as separate from

everything we observe.

Some people believe that God makes the laws of the earth. He gives us control over it and steps back from what happens. Some of us, whether we admit it or not, believe in this idea. We balance between nihilism and cynicism as we try to understand the craziness of the world. People who believe in immanence also face similar thoughts. They often use spiritual bypassing to dodge the hard truths of death and disappointment.

At some point, we must understand that balance in life is key to our survival. We come from spiritual people who viewed nature as proof of a Creator. They also understood that we carry parts of that DNA within us. This makes us active participants in the Creator's world. The Creator is in us and our awareness of the invisible voices and urges inside us is confirmation of that. We are, good brother, creations of the Creator. We can do amazing things, but we have limits. We are indeed little gods, but like robots, we have an expiration date and limitations. You can do great things and have way more power and control over your life than you'll ever know, but even stars die.

With that knowledge, aim to move like a god. Dream big, take risks, and don't let your present stop you from shaping your future. Knowing you aren't here forever means you should consider your legacy. Think about what you want to leave behind for others. This could be something tangible, like a book, building, or organization. It might also be something intangible, like your words or actions. So, avoid being reckless. You are not immortal, and your actions impact others, too. Gods aren't meant to be trapped. So, remember to respect everyone. Acknowledge the divinity in others. If you don't, your power might be taken away for good.

God is in Me

Perspective: Black Liberation Theology

I identify as Christian, but I've also explored many faiths. From Islam to Buddhism, these experiences have broadened my view of God. A key idea for me was the work of James Cone, a black theology scholar. He developed the concept of Black Liberation Theology. This interpretation of the Bible and Christianity is rebellious. It focuses on ideas that challenge traditional views of meekness and false concern. God sees the oppressed, like black people, and wants us to be free. He looks at examples of the Israelites in the Bible. He suggests that God actively saved them from oppression. Black Liberation Theology also honors the strength of African spiritual traditions. This includes spirituals and other types of black music.

If you see yourself as a Christian and strongly support the Bible, this may be tough to think about. Still, I encourage you to explore the African tradition in the black church as a counterpoint. Many black people see the Bible as a tool for today. We feel it's our role to bring its messages to life.

Instead of getting lost in allegorical meanings, we focus on its relevance now. This has allowed us a way to see ourselves in a text and religion that has historically been used to oppress us. I encourage you, as a Black man, to think about how God wants us to be active. This means not just how we see the Word, but also how we treat His people in the world. You should stand up for the oppressed people in your life. This includes children, the elderly, and others who lack the privileges you enjoy. Don't hear the word privilege and freak out though bro. I get it. Even with our burdens, God has blessed us. We should use our powers to help free those around us. Moses was illiterate but was still able to lead his people out of captivity. You might have some disadvantages, but don't give up.

Instead, look to our Black brothers for inspiration. Let's make the most of what we have. Viewing the Bible through a Black lens shows how people overcame challenges to achieve greatness. This perspective can be truly inspiring.

The Black Pill

Treatment

Perspective: Wu

Wei

Every day, I see a video or post from a
relationship guru. They tell men to be valuable
and women to lower their expectations. At first, I
liked the fun chatter and laughter. People
challenged him and shared their ideas. But
soon, I grew to dislike it. I tire of seeing men
sharing it and women criticizing it. I don't
disagree with some of it. I've just watched its
growth for a long time and feel at peace with it
now.

About eleven years ago, I stumbled upon Rollo
Tomasi's seminal hit, *The Rational Male*. I'm
not sure if I found it through a friend in the man-
o-sphere or from my research on young men's
websites. These sites taught skills like
changing tires and other manly activities. I do
know it came into my life during my early
twenties, a crucial time. Like many men who
explore this path, it changed my view on life, for
better and worse. I was in my first adult

relationship. I felt happy to be loved but also uncomfortable with the challenges it brought. In college, I was the loveless guy. I had many friends who were girls. I admired and envied my buddies. They had the women they wanted, including the ones I liked too. I felt like the ugly duckling for much of my life. I often sought validation from women.

When I didn't get it, I felt frustrated and bitter at their choices. College was a constant cycle of the same feelings. Meeting my first girlfriend at 22 felt like a dream come true. I couldn't grasp how to handle someone wanting me so much. It was even harder to cope with the changes that came as my confidence and surroundings improved.

The more confident I felt, the more girls seemed to like me. Also, when I left my usual surroundings, my ugly duckling thoughts felt less real. I felt conflicted because someone loved me, but I felt caged by their possessiveness. When my relationship ended, I turned to the red pill community. I embraced its cynicism and negativity. I focused on becoming the kind of man I admired. I was reading the Rational Male closely. Then, I tried to attract as many women as I could, especially those aged 27 to 29. I spent years reflecting and finding release as I faced my insecurities in my memoir, **Jaded Gems**. A sort of anti-red pill book, it focused on my own issues and explained why I thought they were right. But rather than sell you on why they were wrong, I'll focus on what I learned.

Deep down, I knew I wasn't pessimistic. No matter how much I hurt, I wanted to marry and have kids. Focusing too much on negativity wouldn't help me reach that goal. I focused on what made sense. I worked hard to improve my body and career. I thought that looking better would bring me validation from women and solve my problems.

Everything changed when I realized that seeking validation from others was a trap. I had to concentrate on satisfying my desires and discovering my true self.

For many of us who deal with feeling worthless, it is appealing to embrace red pill ideas. Women in pain often sought quick fixes to their problems. They chased after wealthy men but overlooked how it hurt to be treated like a commodity. For many, especially the younger generation, a moment of self-discovery will come. But this isn't about them. You need to face some truths in your life. It's time to swallow the red pill that's been stuck in your gut. Those truths are simple but heavy, and if taken head-on, can change your life over time. We will call these truths black pill treatments.

Black Pill Truth #1: The only person to blame for your life is you. The only certainty in life is your attitude toward growth and change.

Black Pill Truth #2: Women, just like men, seek what's best for themselves. We don't usually act for others' good if it doesn't help us, too.

Black Pill Truth #3: Controlling your desire for

sex and redirecting that urge towards creative avenues will provide you with a better quality of life than any amount of money, clothing, and other appendages will ever offer.

<u>Black Pill Truth #4</u>: Masculinity is about action. But that action should feel natural and effortless. You can't force success and the outcomes you desire to appear. Start by setting your intention. Then, work towards your goal.

Finally, make peace with the outcome.

You might be wondering how to achieve this. It can be tough when you see your peers, celebrities, and others enjoying the life you desire. Wu-wei means effortless action. Let me explain it in simple terms. You need to know that, no matter what others say, skills are often mastered in a flow state. In this state, a person lets go of their thoughts and embraces what happens. You can't control others, no matter how much you try to influence them. It should feel easy and reflect who you are. So, accept two facts: You can't choose when or if you'll get what you want. Consider if what you want holds true value.

A key moment in my life happened after my first relationship. I spoke with my mentor, who was also in an unfulfilling long-term relationship. As we drove and talked, he said I should be the kind of man who could accept not having things I valued, like a wife and kids. In his late 30s, he was the kind of guy I wanted to be. Yet, he showed me that not getting what you want isn't as bad as pushing for it and staying unhappy. That was a far worse fate, one that spoke to a losing mindset, and one that affected more than me. No matter your age, remember that inaction is still a choice. Sometimes, not pursuing what we want leads us to what we truly need. You can't force women to respect you. Criticizing them for their choices doesn't help and shows a twisted mindset. Your beliefs and values show your thoughts. Follow your interests. You'll help the world more that way. Don't worry about what others think. My mentor made me see something RZA wrote in his book, **The Tao of the Wu**. He told his partner that she once saved him. But now, he feels complete on his own. Our goal as men and leaders is to be self-sufficient. But we must also understand the importance of community. Having a helpmate is key, but allowing it to come to us is essential.

Force vs Power

To this day, the dynamic of force vs power
remains one of my favorite ideas to ponder and
sit with. I found two explanations. The first is
from Professor Jared Sexton at the University
of California. He wrote about it in his book,
Black Men Black Feminism: Lucifer's Nocturne.
The second explanation is in David Hawkins'
book, *Power vs Force*. Jared claims that black
men often use force to dominate women. They
often realize that they feel powerless in their
own lives and in their partners' lives.
David Hawkins describes force and power
through a scale of emotions. Our lowest
emotions rely on force, but our highest selves
use power to create positive change.

To explain each in detail would require more
time and nuance than we have, but I'll do my
best to give you the jaded gems. When we are
at our best, we control our vices. We channel
that energy into healthy habits. We also
manage what we see, hear, and say. This
makes us more appealing and helps others
want to listen to us. Power emphasizes positive
emotions like courage, love, and patience. To
become a better version of yourself, you should

embrace these traits deeply. Make them part of your thoughts and feelings. We often think others should see the world like we do. But forcing agreement only adds to the tension today. Leaders and movements that lead us to destruction often tap into our fears. They also trigger feelings of guilt that arise from these fears.

It sounds like it shouldn't work the way it does, but the more you try to get others to think or act the way you do or to see things how you do, the more you end up losing power and respect.

To show the energy of a man who controls his emotions, let go of regret, guilt, anger, vengeance, and ego. Instead, embrace courage, acceptance, love, and more. Power isn't just in persuasion. Peace and understanding help a person feel in control of their destiny. This makes them less likely to try to control others.

Traffic Over Truth-What To Do When Lies Run Faster and Further

If you're like me, you have strong feelings about the opinions shared online. Some are necessary, but most are distracting and dehumanizing. They often present all-or-nothing views on race and sex. You see, hear, and internalize this noise. At first, you feel it's your duty to respond on social media and in group chats. You think it will fight the wave of misinformation and dishonesty. But remember, people don't change their minds because something is true. They change when they hear the same truth often.

If you're reading this, you may be a Black man wanting to model good Black masculinity. You want to be the type of man you saw in your family, on teams, or on TV that modeled positive attributes of masculinity. Allowing half-truths to spread feels wrong, yet we live in a time when a few loud voices push their version of reality, even when evidence contradicts it. Today, the truth is what people hear most from those who think alike. To protect your peace, accept that people only embrace ideas that fit their reality. Challenging them without understanding can lead you to frustration.

For example, I've often found myself misunderstood on social media. Colleagues misinterpret my posts or comments and label me as they choose. It doesn't matter if I speak in a straightforward manner or with skill. Some people cling to their own truth. Many men grow cynical about women. Many women see more negative men than positive ones due to their experiences. Instead of feeling anger or shame, I chose to let people believe what they want. I redirected my energy toward my audience instead of confronting them. It makes sense to respond to what we hear most, so I decided to step back from that game.

Some might suggest adopting a stoic mindset, but there are limits. If you feel pressured to stay stoic like I do, try this two-part method: attachment and detachment. This involves journaling your thoughts and taking breaks from social media. The algorithm causes dysfunction. Even if you try to curate your feed, it will still show triggering posts. On your journey, try not to absorb too many thoughts from others.

📖 📖 Bonus Materials for Your

Journey You're not alone in

this.

As you reflect, grow, and heal, I want to offer you tools that go beyond these pages. I've prepared a digital collection of resources—journaling prompts, audio messages, worksheets, and exclusive content—to support you wherever you are.

📱 📱 Scan the QR Code Below

References

Browder, A. T. (1992). *Nile Valley contributions to civilization: Exploding the myths*. Institute of Karmic Guidance.

Cone, J. H. (1969). *Black theology and Black power*. Orbis Books.

Delany, M. R. (1852). *The condition, elevation, emigration, and destiny of the colored people of the United States*. Retrieved from https://docsouth.unc.edu/neh/delany/delany.html

Gilligan, C. (1982). *In a different voice: Psychological theory and women's development*. Harvard University Press.

Hillman, J. (1996). *The soul's code: In search of character and calling*. Random House.

Ichazo, O. (1970s). *Enneagram of personality types*. Arica School.

Jones, J., & Mosher, W. D. (2013). *Fathers' involvement with their children: United States, 2006–2010* (National Health Statistics Reports No. 71). National Center for Health Statistics. https://www.cdc.gov/nchs/data/nhsr/nhsr071.p

df

Mbiti, J. S. (1969). *African religions and philosophy* (pp. 108–112). Heinemann.

Morehouse, M. (2008). African diaspora theory: Here, there, and everywhere. *The Journal of Pan-African Studies*, 2(4), 86–104.

Rasi, T. (2013). *The rational male*. Independently published.

Sidanius, J., & Pratto, F. (1999). *Social dominance: An intergroup theory of social hierarchy and oppression* (pp. 45–67). Cambridge University Press.

Sexton, J. (2020). *Black men, Black feminism: Lucifer's nocturne* (pp. 88–91). Palgrave Macmillan.

White, R. E., & Carlson, S. M. (2016). The Batman effect: Improving perseverance in young children. *Child Development*, 87(5), 1202–1211.
https://doi.org/10.1111/cdev.12590

Wilber, K. (2006). *Introduction to integral theory and practice: IOS basic and the AQAL map*. Integral Institute.

Wilson, A. N. (1993). *The falsification of Afrikan consciousness: Eurocentric history, psychiatry and the politics of white

supremacy* (pp. 23–39). Afrikan World
Infosystems.

About the Author

Samuel Wright is an Atlanta-based author, educator, and speaker with a passion for storytelling that sheds light on social and cultural challenges in today's ever-evolving world. A graduate of Fort Valley State University, where he earned both a Bachelor of Science in Education and a Master of Arts in History, Wright now serves as a school administrator by day and an adjunct professor by night. His written contributions span publications like Hip Hop DX and Hip Hop Wired, and he shares his editorial insights and interviews through his Substack, Solomon's Soul, under the pen name Solomon Hillfleet. In his work, Wright strives to engage readers in critical conversations about modern masculinity and identity. His latest release, Jaded Gems, is a poignant memoir collection addressing the struggles that men face today, from hypermasculinity to vulnerability. His forthcoming title, For Black Men Who Need Therapy and Never Got It, confronts the urgent mental health crisis and offers thoughtful solutions.

Wright draws literary inspiration from luminaries such as Richard Wright, James Baldwin, and Carson McCullers. Through his writings, he seeks to illuminate intersectional experiences and inspire dialogue that transcends generations.